Seals

Seals

Charles Rotter

THE CHILD'S WORLD®, INC.

Published in the United States of America by The Child's World®, Inc.
PO Box 326
Chanhassen, MN 55317-0326
800-599-READ
www.childsworld.com

Product Manager Mary Berendes
Editor Katherine Stevenson
Designer Mary Berendes
Contributor Bob Temple

Photo Credits
© 2000 Barbara Gerlach/Dembinsky Photo Assoc. Inc.: 19 (small photo)
© 2001 Brandon D. Cole: 6, 15
© Daniel J. Cox/naturalexposures.com: 9, 16, 29, 30
© 1996 Dusty Perin/Dembinsky Photo Assoc. Inc.: 24
© 1999 Kevin Schafer: cover, 20
© 2000 Kevin Schafer: 13 (small photo), 23
© 2001 Kim Westerskov/Stone: 2
© Marilyn & Maris Kazmers/Sharksong: 10 (both photos), 13, 26
© Wyb Hoek/Marine Mammal Images: 19 (main photo)

Library of Congress Cataloging-in-Publication Data
Rotter, Charles.
Seals / by Charles Rotter.
p. cm.
ISBN 1-56766-891-7 (lib. bdg. : alk. paper)
1. Seals (Animals)—Juvenile literature. [1. Seals (Animals)]
I. Title.
QL737.P63 R68 2001
599.79—dc21
00-011132

On the cover...

Front cover: This baby harp seal lives in Quebec, Canada.
Page 2: This Weddell seal is breaking through some slushy ice on the ocean's surface.

Table of Contents

The water of the ocean looks murky and deep. Suddenly a flash of light appears on the surface—and then disappears. Was it just a trick of the light? Or was it something else? The flash appears again, a little closer. This time you can see that it is an animal coming to the surface and diving quickly away. What is this fast-moving animal? It's a seal!

What Are Seals?

Seals are a type of **mammal.** Mammals are animals that have hair on their bodies, have warm blood, and feed their babies milk from their bodies. People are another type of mammal. Seals also belong to a group of animals called **pinnipeds.** Pinnipeds are animals that have flippers instead of arms and legs. Walruses and sea lions are pinnipeds, too.

This Weddell seal lives in Antarctica. ⇒

Seals have smooth bodies covered with sleek fur. They have round, dark eyes and whiskers on their faces. Seals feel with their whiskers the way we feel with our fingers. They use their whiskers to find food and avoid bumping into things in the dark water.

All seals have four flippers. The front flippers are short, with claws on the "fingers." The rear flippers are more like paddles. Seals use their flippers to swim and change direction in the water. On land, the flippers are useless. Seals must wriggle and flop to get from place to place.

⇐ *Main photo:* This northern elephant seal is scratching its head with its front flipper.
Small photo: Here you can see the rear flippers of another northern elephant seal.

How Are Seals and Sea Lions Different?

Many people think that seals and sea lions are the same animal. From a distance, these two creatures look a lot alike. But up close, you can see big differences. Seals are often much smaller than sea lions. They also have shorter bodies and shorter flippers.

One of the easiest ways to tell seals and sea lions apart is to look for their ears. Sea lions have ears sticking out from their heads. Seals do not, except for one type called the *fur seal*.

Unlike seals, this Galapagos sea lion has ⇒
a long snout and ears that stick out.

Seals and sea lions also swim differently. Seals swim almost like fish or dolphins, pumping their rear flippers up and down to move through the water. Sea lions, however, flap their front flippers like a bird flapping its wings. Their front flippers pull them through the water. Sea lions can also turn their rear flippers forward to help them "walk" on land. Seals must flop along on their bellies.

This harbor seal is curious about the photographer. ⇒

Are There Different Types of Seals?

There are about 27 different kinds, or **species,** of seals. Some seals are small, cute, and furry. Others are large animals with strange faces. *Elephant seals* got their name from the older male's strange nose—it looks like an elephant's trunk! Elephant seals are the largest type of seal. Some males can grow to weigh over 5,000 pounds.

⇐ This large male elephant seal is making lots of noise.

Harp seals are named after the harp-shaped ring of color on their back. Their babies are born completely white and are often pictured in nature magazines. Male *hooded seals* have a "hood" of skin they can fill with air to make themselves look bigger. *Leopard seals* have spotted coats, much like the big cats after which they are named. Leopard seals have a wide mouth and very sharp teeth for grabbing their dinner.

Main photo: You can see part of the harp shape on this harp seal's back. ⇒
Small photo: This baby harp seal lives in Canada.

Seals usually live along coastlines, especially in colder seas. While some seals live in warmer climates, most live in the Arctic or Antarctic. One reason they can live in cold seas is that they are covered with thick fur. The fur helps keep in their body heat, protecting them from the cold water. Seals also have a layer of fat called **blubber** under their skin. The blubber also helps hold in their body heat.

⇐ This female harp seal has surfaced to breathe through a hole in the ice in Quebec, Canada. The air is so cold that ice has formed on her whiskers, but she doesn't seem to mind.

What Do Seals Eat?

Seals are **carnivores,** which means they hunt and eat other animals. They especially like to eat fish. They also eat other sea creatures such as shrimp, crabs, and octopuses. Some seals, such as leopard seals, eat penguins and even other seals.

Leopard seals are known for being very aggressive hunters. Penguins are their favorite food. Typically, a leopard seal chases and grabs a penguin in the water and thrashes it back and forth. With its fierce strength and incredible speed, the seal can even jump onto the ice to grab its victim.

Main photo: This leopard seal is resting in Antarctica. ⇒
Small Photo: You can see how large this leopard seal's mouth is when it yawns.

Seals often group together in large numbers. They leave the water to rest on land and lounge in the sun. Male seals are called **bulls.** Each bull claims an area of land, called a **territory,** as his own. The bull lets females into his territory, but he doesn't let other males in. If a bull enters another male's territory, a fight often occurs. The winner of the fight gets to keep the territory.

⇐ These male northern elephant seals are fighting over a territory on a California beach.

What Are Baby Seals Like?

Female seals, or **cows,** have their babies on land. Most cows have just one baby, called a **pup,** at a time. The mother takes care of her pup for several weeks. The pup drinks its mother's milk and grows quickly.

Newborn baby seals can swim, but they are not very strong swimmers. Before they can take care of themselves, they must grow stronger. They must also be fat enough to float easily in the water. After about a month, the pup is big enough to live on its own. The mother leaves, and the young seal must now catch its own dinner.

⇐ This newborn northern elephant seal is staying very close to its mother. They both are resting on a California beach.

Do Seals Have Many Enemies?

Just as some animals are food for seals, seals are food for other animals. On northern coastlines, seals must watch out for polar bears. Sharks and killer whales also attack and eat seals.

Seals' biggest enemy, however, is people. For many years, people have killed seals to eat their meat or to make clothes from their fur. Some types of seals are in danger of being wiped out completely.

Hawaiian monk seals like this one are in danger of dying out. ⇒

There are now many laws to protect seals from people. Hunting is still allowed, but only in certain places and at certain times. But our world is very big. Laws passed in one part of the world cannot always protect animals in another part.

Seals are fascinating animals. Like all wild creatures, they are an important part of life on Earth. If they can be protected, we can enjoy seeing them swim and play for years to come.

Glossary

blubber (BLUB-ber)
Blubber is a thick layer of fat that most ocean mammals have beneath their skin. The blubber keeps the animals warm in the cold ocean water.

bulls (BULLZ)
Male seals are called bulls. Bull seals sometimes fight with each other.

carnivores (KAR-nih-vorz)
Carnivores are animals that eat the meat of other animals. Seals are carnivores.

cows (KOWZ)
Female seals are called cows. Cows have just one baby at a time.

mammal (MAM-mull)
Mammals are animals that have warm blood, have hair or fur, and feed their babies milk from their bodies. Seals are mammals, and so are people.

pinnipeds (PIN-nih-pedz)
Pinnipeds are mammals that have fin-like flippers instead of legs or arms. Seals are pinnipeds.

pup (PUP)
A baby seal is called a pup. Usually a seal mother has only one pup at a time.

species (SPEE-sheez)
A species is a separate kind of an animal. There are about 27 different species of seals.

territory (TEHR-ih-tor-ee)
A territory is an area of land that an animal claims as its own. Male seals claim and defend a territory.

Web Sites

http://www.seaworld.org/Pinnipeds/introduction.html

http://www.greenchannel.com/tec/species/species.htm

http://school.discovery.com/homeworkhelp/worldbook/atozscience/s/498340.html

http://animal.discovery.com/cams/seal/seal.html

http://www.tmmc.org/pinniped.htm